T0103748

LOVE GIFTS

Poems

LOVE GIFTS

Tanure Ojaide

AFRICAN HERITAGE PRESS
New York • Lagos • London
2013

AFRICAN HERITAGE PRESS

NEW YORK
PO BOX 1433
NEW ROCHELLE, NY 10802
USA

LAGOS
PO BOX 14452
IKEJA, LAGOS
NIGERIA

TEL: (Toll Free) 855-247-7737; 914-481-8488
FAX: 914-481-8489
ahp@africanheritagepress.com
www.africanheritagepress.com

First Edition, African Heritage Press, 2013

Copyright © African Heritage Press, 2013

All rights reserved. No part of this publication may be reproduced or transmitted in any form or by any means, electronic or mechanical, without permission in writing from the publisher.

Library of Congress catalog number: 2013932978

Ojaide, Tanure

Cover Design: Bruce Onabrakpeya

Distributors: African Books Collective, www.africanbookscollective.com

The characters and events in this collection are fictitious. Any similarity to persons or situations is coincidental and not intended by the author.

ISBN: 978-0-9790858-9-5

Dedication

For the special muse, who possessed and inspired
the minstrel to sing these human "songs."

I am ashamed
to call this love human
and afraid of God
to call it divine

* * *

You dance inside my chest,
where no one sees you,

but . . . I do, and that
sight becomes this art.

(Rumi)

Contents

1. The Landmark

I freeze the landmark moment to run and rerun
when solitude breaks in to torture me with hell
by flaunting you at my face an inescapable spell.
And so every day now I drive you so leisurely
through potholed roads with the annoying spate
of police checkpoints to drop you at the junction
to take a taxi home where you'll then be cooped;
daily I relish the singular beatitude of the visit.
Evening comes to seize you by right of custom
and I surrender you to the imperial power of night
that must swathe and ravish you out of my sight.
I look forward to when you'll be stuck with me
in a defiant storm that will drown the entire day;
I will rename you, chant your name to the stars
and at dawn's tender call walk abreast to the river
to sit in a row boat and not mind the world
while sailing with the morning currents towards
the sea waking from dreams of unfathomable love
and waiting to bless sojourners with divine breath.
You'll then be the true bird you are, bright and
beautiful sailing smoothly with freedom of flight
denied when I drop you to beat the nightly curfew;
I suffer insomniac dark hours praying for the next trip.
I keep rerunning the landmark moment in your absence
to survive the tortures of solitude, calling you for rescue.

2. If I Were

If I were endowed with the craft of a spell, I would
summon her to my presence—no parrot resists corn before it!

If I had the gift of seeing through the future, I would
pronounce her name among the avatars of hearts;

if I had the magic to change things to my desires,
she would be my first act as a miracle minstrel.

if the divine ones asked me what prayer I wanted heeded,
her wellbeing would be all I need from the bottom of my heart;

if I were to meet a generous djinn in my wandering,
I would mount her on my gift horse and ride away.

if the day wanted to treat me with a spectacle, I would
open my eyes only to the pleasure of her beauty;

if the long night held me in its cell till dawn, she would
be the hope that crowns the dreamer's search for freedom.

if the sky threatened the land with a severe face, I know
she would be the rain that breaks the season's drought;

and if I had been struck dumb by the dreary landscape
she would surely be the song that breaks the vast silence.

3. Love Lesson

You are teaching me how to be satisfied
with a morsel and not the whole to myself.
To you, sharing brings fulfillment even if
we receive only crumbs of our tall wishes—
there's nothing like an appetite that won't
still ask for more and so half or full will do.
I cannot have all of you, nor you all of me;
that reality grabs either of us by the wrist.

Seeing me always trembling in your presence,
why would you ask me to take on another?
I was confused by your counsel and knew not
whether you were testing the tenacity of my heart.
But it seems you care not in sharing, as long
as you get enough to fill your simple appetite.
I search for jealousy in your dictionary, the bad
blood in sharing rather than hoarding to oneself

but see nothing there to contradict your nature.
Where is the notorious green spirit that drives
folks into insanity once their partner is shared?
Where's the yellow monster that gnaws at the flesh
unrelenting that psychologists often warn against?
What deity blessed you with this intriguing gift
I had thought non-human but normal with you?
Who won't deny others what you want for yourself?

Now, how do we maintain and strengthen this possession
which you do not want to keep tight entirely to yourself?
Can love survive sharing like a ripe tasty pumpkin
or bread broken to pieces and still fill all concerned?
You are teaching me a lesson I had thought impossible
for humans to fathom in their vacuous hunger to possess:
communion allows for a happier experience, and
so to be more human share what we love the most!

4. The Uwara Suite

I

An evergreen tree flourishes in the desert
and, of course, folks wonder how possible—
nobody knows the wine-dark undercurrent
perennially sustaining the fortunate one.

II

The forefinger stands out from the lot
and many wonder why so effortlessly—
they know not its natural endowment;
the favorite comes first in the crowd.

III

The *uwara* stands beside multitudes in the forest
and maintains its cool despite assaulting storms—
she who is my uwara carries abundant resilience;
the confident one inspires victory against all odds.

* uwara: a tall slender tree that in Urhobo mythology is symbolic
of female beauty and constant comportment. It is the counterfoil
of *akpobrisi*, a male tree that is symbolic of tyranny and diabolic
power.

5. Through You

Through you I knew Nyerhovwo* closely
even though I never set eyes on him any day,
and I couldn't but share this pain with you.
Stung by the news, he wasn't only your son's
friend but also every youth with zestful life.
You must be reflecting on your own son's fate
as of all wearing the frail fabric of humanity
prone to savage ambush and a sudden fall—
one goat's sacrifice a fearsome warning to others!

You had been assisting on how he could enter
the university and study to take care of himself.
And suddenly on a World Cup match day, woken
from afternoon nap, he joined age-mates to play
out their tall dreams before the real match began.
And without a hint of ailment, the vivacious one
collapsed and spirited away by the invisible ogre.
Death cannot be a lie, and the news spread cold fever
to all who knew Nyerhovwo. Even lightning forewarns,
but not this day's demise; deft ambush that caught parents
and friends by the wrong foot, none escaped the cold grip.

Hopes had bloomed when parents named their son
Nyerhovwo, believing their prayers had been heeded.
But what prayers did they say that unknowingly hacked
down the young iroko already towering above brushes?
In Nyerhovwo's birth, God heeded whose prayers,
the parents' or the child's? Or did God heed some
unheard prayers? And what if the divine had nothing
to do with the comforting vanity of self-serving parents?

But death cannot be a lie! The news spread cold;
the fever benumbed you the entirety of many days.
You condemned why wild fire chose the green leaf
over dry leaves in abundance in the interminable

forest to devour to fill its burning frenzy at any cost.
I told you the mystery of life and the inscrutable nature
of the sagely one who makes and unmakes at will.
We reflect on this loss for long because through you
I knew Nyerhovwo closely, sharing the feverish cold.

Who is so stricken by the mortal ambush of youth
will defend life with all the resources at her disposal;
who takes as her own son another's lost one
will carry a stranger's crushing load to relieve another!
Who challenges the aborted growth of the iroko
will freely bless all to attain their desired heights;
who is capable of suffering this deep wound for another
has a heart to save others from the tyranny of tears!
And I share with you, tender heart, this memorial song.

* Nyerhovwo, the shortened form of Oghenenyerhovwo in
  Urhobo literally means God has heeded (our) prayers.

6. There

There
you watch *Africa Magic**
an hourly addiction for many
or *Super Story**
on Thursday nights with light

here
I am racked in fantasies
of the interdependence of men and women
and the complementarity of light and dark
a human narrative

and when you switch channels
to Chelsea or Real Madrid
scoring fabulous goals
with hat tricks

I will still be staring at your photo
an untiring sport
waiting for you medicine-woman
to turn your magical attention here.

* *Africa Magic* is a DSTV channel showing only African movies.
* *Super Story* is a soap opera on Nigeria Television Authority on
   Thursday nights.

7. Over Here

Over here, it's neither dream nor vision,
the type in which the *sokugo** possesses you
to be a wanderer in an unending wilderness;
nor the sort in which the more water you throw at
the fire-engulfed victim the more irate the flames.
No, it's not launching into a compulsive storm
that the rest of the world sees as a suicidal venture
but to you proffers only solace rather than peril.
What transpires here is neither dream nor vision
of a fantasy that belies life as one knows it.
This is not a dream or vision of flight
on the back of a falcon coasting the skies
over a shark-infested ocean and singing.
This is a spell of unknown proportion whose
words only the medicine-woman can chant
to bring the world of insanity to normalcy;
only she possesses the power to calm the waves,
put out the voluptuous flames, bring to an end
the civil war that ravages the entire polity.
This is not magical realism—a man bleeding
from love, a woman holding a man on a leash;
a colony of mute parrots with signs banished
and tongues and eyes sick from disuse.
A minstrel cries from a devastating fever
to the medicine-woman out there gathering
healing chants from a garden of secret herbs,
and daring to heal one not given a chance
and so cocksure of her curative craft.

---

* *sokugo*: "the wandering disease" that makes one a compulsive
  wanderer. Made popular by Cyprian Ekwensi in his *Burning Grass*.

8. I Will Deify You

I

I will deify you in the temple of my faith—
I perform miracles invoking your blessed name.

I will humanize you with a praise-song—
you bestir the street with longing and collision.

I have tripped over street blocks in daylight,
I have made a sanctuary of your presence;

you surely inhabit a singular planet
whose constellation lights my world;

I see you daily as I perform mundane tasks
and you summon me with a possessing gaze.

For the anonymity of the storm you stir,
flameless conflagration that transforms all

I will humanize you with a praise-song;
I will deify you in the temple of my faith.

II

I have searched for tropes and epithets to paint your portrait
but you always appear dressed more elegantly than my find.

Of course, I rule out colorful birds and flowers
that have been exhausted on pedestrian personages.

I have been sculpting a chair to sit you in a dominion
but the throne you deserve tasks my talent for more craft.

I have been sketching the beauty and grace of your face
but have not come up with the picture of your nobility.

I have been composing and rehearsing a song for my favorite
but it comes without the facility of a flowing stream in flood.

I have searched the recesses of day and night
but have not found what beats you in the imagination—

you are the most creative of arts in your genre
and the imagination cannot embellish you further.

III
The one whose lone number surpasses thousands
the one whose dish fills all desires and wish for no other

the one waiting decades for exceeds expectations of centuries
the one whose spectacle subsumes every possible beauty

the one whose attention possesses the entire being
the one the pilgrim finds at the end of the pilgrimage

she's the full moon whose light outshines countless stars
she's the rainbow possessing every shade of colors

she's the one whose tongue is the song of the day
she's the favorite I serenade with the song of songs

and once you come to her you have found a refuge
once you arrive at hers you are done with wandering.

9. If It Were Not for You

If it were not for you so lucent, thousands of stars
wouldn't be shining this bright to gain my attention

if it were not for you so vivacious, every new day
wouldn't be breaking with such youthful zest

if it were not for thousands of miles between us, the crow
wouldn't be bearing tirelessly to me the message of hope

if it were not for you guardian spirit, I wouldn't be
sleepwalking in a storm chasing monsters with sticks

if it were not for you there a rock, I wouldn't be
overflying the shark-infested ocean to my home

if it were not for the generous spell of the muse,
the minstrel wouldn't be the fortunate celebrant

but because of you the rest of the world refuses
to forgive my inattention to its serious business.

10. When She Gave the Word

When she gave the word
more than her body in its effulgence
he accepted the task
of watchman to forever
keep any intruder out of the way
hold fire inside his frame
to cleanse the charge
without hurt
bathe the companion
with the Ethiope's cool water
always be the sweeper
of the temple at dawn
prune the garden
of thorns and needless growth
and never complain
and not wait to be called upon
to keep the fire burning
with wood from the haunted forest
across the deep river
full from perennial floods.
When she gave the word
more than her haloed body
he knew his task in return.

11. You Are

You are

the evergreen
whose assured shade cools me wherever there's heat

the compass
that guides me in the wilderness to the direction of my desire

the fragrance
that makes me favorite of all that come my way

the lamp
with which I find my way through the dark

the oil
whose special property softens any hardship I encounter

you are

the endless song
I sing to celebrate the blessings of life.

12. They Begin Tendentiously

They begin tendentiously
chameleon-wise one reluctant step after another

until so sure-footed
they move with the gracefulness of the giraffe

a rhythmic flow so natural
every step dissolves distance

and what a time it takes
for dew breakers to wait till noon

and curfew breakers
to keep vigil till dawn!

"One foot at a time"
sings the initiate

and with practiced steps
the adept makes no error in the rites

like the shared mystery
between the monkey and hundreds of branches

from tendentious leaps
to the facility of the forester.

We all begin the same way:
one clumsy step after another

the totem bird tottering on one leg
before the two legs can dance and fly

aiming at the agility of the adept
with no insecure move

as medicine-woman and minstrel
take one assured step after another

in the flowing rhythm of veteran travelers
their destination a known fact to both.

13. You Have Taken Steps

You have taken several steps forward
and in another mood others backwards;

you stood in the same place wondering where
to proceed: back to drudgery or forward to ecstasy.

"But everyone has doubts at one point or another,"
you say, but not after crossing seven rivers

or returning from the feared haunted forest
with the firewood that always burns bright

as you now have for your spectacular hearth;
assurance of a blazing season despite cold.

You know not how multi-tasking from dawn to dusk
has steeled you against ambushes and false alarms,

you know not how charlatans sought you
with promises you saw through in their emptiness;

you cannot waver forever a reed in the delta tide
in which you have grown strong in four decades;

you are now tough enough to absorb storms and floods,
lose yourself in the ecstasy of the journey's adventure.

You wavering on the two-some journey,
it's my turn to shake you like a reed in the tide,

make you shake in my non-malarial fever
with a possessing spirit tugging at my heartstrings.

14. Inevitably

Inevitably, the cat leaves its domestic home
for the forest, as the python slides into the river,
to enjoy the legendary beauty of the wilds.

Naturally, every snake would look to casting off
its old skin to live forever young and beautiful,
reinvent itself in the new life the body requires.

Who has the resources to be beautiful and free
to relish inner and outer landscapes of contentment
and let the chance pass for drudgery and enslavement?

Naturally, we want to cast off our age
to relive the possibilities of a second youth
and wear the beautiful cotton of rejuvenation.

Inevitably, the river finds its destined lake or sea
to relieve itself of anguish and lonely wandering
and be one with a mate vast and deep; voluptuous.

And so we seek journeys into fresh vistas,
seek new diets of belated brides and grooms
that make life a delight to live every existence.

15. See

See what you have made me into
all this while
we have been laughing together!
I have become

a king
whose stunning queen
extols monastic virtues
even as she wants to produce heirs

a watchman
of a human treasure extraordinary
that I cover in darkness and daylight
and want for myself without stealing

a chieftain
whose unchanging customs
lay down heartless rules
I am sworn to break

a minstrel
whose generous muse
praises Plato's restrained love
even as she stokes my unconditional love for her.

In the short while
we have been laughing together
you have so transformed me
now see what you have made me!

16. Three Times I Call

Three times I call
three times you answer
your voice floating
from dream to reality
and reality to dream
I watchman at my post
with a secret task.

You whose trenchant voice
flows from chamber music
to the trenches of silence
there's enough serenading
to possess you medicine-woman
to throw dust at the eyes
of dancing masqueraders
tyrannizing the arena with grunts.

And here I am devoted to
building a throne for a queen
picking from here and there
the property of tailor-ants
to make the queen
free from multiple shackles
that bind her in an institution
that believes in compelling all
to fall into unreasonable line
and also believes in torture
administered by patriarchs.
Now I have to transfer her
into a dominion of smiles.

I will ride in the chariot
you mount to gallop out there
from the dark stable
present you to the people
ransomed from a bride-price's

sellout in the traditional court
and indulge you in the dream
you could not sleep to live out
but now given a mansion
to live in a fantasy dominion
where neither cowries nor corals
matter to a smiling face chatting
with the singer of your pageant.

Medicine-woman and queen,
here in one big heart
you live in the throne
whose value surpasses properties
and priced above diamonds
the sustainer of life
in partnership with a free spirit
that knows life as a sharing experience
be it of pumpkin or laughter,
sour loaf or headaches
for mates that happen to each other;
two sovereigns in one dominion
employing each other's resources
together building an empire
of virtual contentment.

Three times I call
three times you answer
your voice floating
from dream to reality
and reality to dream
I watchman at my post
with a secret task.

17. Touch

At your wish we sit apart
sovereigns in respective thrones
and not spouses clasping hands—
two stars beaming light at each other
and caring less about physical touch
as if that would make them collide
and fall into irreconcilable spheres.

Now and then a chance touch,
light but so poignant the warmth.
In the two thrones beside the other
a hearth fans the two a humid swath
in the season's rainy weather;
unpremeditated heart's content.

Only once after the most anticipated tryst
prepared with the care of a state visit
and the security of practical intelligence
did we clasp in embrace behind curtains
in the afternoon dim light of Power Holdings*
proffering courtesies to two pilgrims
who have made sacrifices to make it.

And the last touch, a preamble to
flouting catholic rules of separateness
I rise from my throne and my hands stroke
your brilliant necklace, the sleek Nefertiti neck
sweeping down towards your breasts
and you watching anxiously and silently
and I not daring enough to go all the way
to squeeze the two luscious landmarks
that certainly brought reciprocal silence;
a stage in the journey; another beginning.

---

* Power Holdings: Power Holdings Company of Nigeria; state
  electricity company notorious for frequent blackouts.

18. On This Dawn

On this dawn I choose to walk alone
and chat in silence with my bride of dawn
but my son insists on also accompanying me.
I feel *our* privacy violated but still go on the walk
and so with my secret companion ready and in tow
with every step I take, every gaze I shoot into the air
from home through the neighborhood walkways
and back, another intense but invisible presence
for an hour to spruce up the day; my good luck charm.
A dog that knows me by my scent still barks loud
and I cover my invisible partner, the stranger around.
The dew-drenched lawns invite *us* to lounge there,
take a break from work and play for a change.
The flowers on the way with their fresh fragrance
hold *us* spellbound to relish their beauty and aroma.
There's no shadow, tall or short, to give out
my companion to those gossiping to stay relevant.
In response to the choral ensemble of dawn's livery,
we nod to the polyrhythmic celebration of life
despite the threatening distance of a vast void.
And engrossed in the company, I wouldn't have
waved back to passersby who must have observed
what a different person from the one they knew.

19. I Trip

I trip as if it is not daylight
and I am not looking at where I am going.

My bifocal eyes have no vision of reality;
they are busily engaged in path-finding elsewhere.

Tell a man who is seeking love in a wilderness
or one who is pained by love in a blooming garden

to meet a diviner to prepare him a healing potion
and none will read between the double lines—

the figure foreshadowing the body;
dusk standing coyly between night and day!

The egg carries the promise of hatching a new life
as the ripe fruit goes back to the seed of long ago

and I hide in the interstices of day and night
invoking my guardian spirit to take me through chaos.

I will be at the crossroads of deafening traffic
giving out to neither light nor dark what I owe to love.

Of course, there's no phantom with this shadow
since beside me a figure glows and moves silently.

No wonder I trip as if it is not daylight
and I am not looking at where I am going

because of one that nobody else sees
but who walks erect in every passage of mine.

20. All Around Me

All around me so musical
I am the compulsive musician

every experience a musical theme
I rest not all day immersed in magic

every silence a pause integral to the piece
all cries wave-lash into a crescendo

my life a polyrhythmic movement
my breathing a syncopating stream

all around me and all in me
intuitive music that plays on

all my thoughts musical forays
all I do and do not do fresh notes

my longings, fantasies musical
my ecstasy, my blues all musical

a broken monody in solitude
a phantom duet in her company

her magical acts my transformation
all around me and in me musical

every touch resonates a melody
every tryst a musical event

I cannot help singing and dancing
because everything around musical

she has so tuned me to herself
I am the music as she the music

everything in and around me so musical
my body is a self-playing harp

every experience so musical
we are the music of life.

21. If Others Had

If others had a fraction of your effortless poise
they would strut like peacocks in a country of chickens

if they had a quarter of your endowment from above
they would boast of their extraordinary fortune

if they had a shadow of your divine figure
they would want to be worshiped by every person

if they possessed apprentice experience of your magic
they would turn others into beasts and be the only humans

if they were covered with a few shreds of your laurel
they would not allow anybody rest from their self-exhibition

if they had something close to your large sparkling eyes
they would not answer greetings because of their class

if they had a measure of your lucent face and beauty spots
they would crown themselves queens of their self-conceit

if they had a pinhead of the rabbit wit of your brains
they would assume a divine accent and never do wrong

if they wore a piece of your mane by right of a lioness
they would shout impossible orders at partners to obey

if they had a partial view of your spectacular elevation
they would look down with scorn at the rest of us

if they had a faint echo of your laughter and its ring
they would make the rest of the world miserable

if they had a parcel of your Mami Wata's dominion
they would drown their worshipers in depths of tears

if others kept the muse's fire in their hearts
they would burn rather than heal the minstrel.

22. Nobody Knows

Nobody knows the radical revolution
that these regular faces plot in daylight

nobody knows the intense fire
burning inside without the least smoke

nobody knows the fierce undercurrent
in the graceful flow of the Ethiope

nobody knows the long dream
in their wakeful hours of daily tasks

eyes open waiting to devour any spectacle
but nobody sees the great masquerade dancing

ears keenly wait to catch the tongue loose
but nobody hears the eloquent dialogue of freedom

nobody sees milk fill the coconut
nobody ever hears the tortoise fart

only they bear witness
to their festive home-warming

and since nobody knows
they relish the private planet they have to themselves.

23. You Don't Have to Look Out

You don't have to look out
to see her
the presence felt
there she is
a lamp on a hilltop
the tall palm of the landscape
you do not look out
wherever you turn
every breathing moment
she's there to see
beauty radiating
from every cardinal point
compelling presence
she listening to the endless song
I sing her
she follows me a heartbeat
her silence
a stream of musical notes
I weave to sing
her tongue
companion in a lonely road
she's always in my chest
always with me
and I don't need to look out
to see her
need no lamp or sunlight
to see her
I serenade with songs.
Blessed is she
who tasks the master artist's talent
blessed is she
who exhausts the Maker's resources
blessed is she
I see without looking out
so blessed is she
I see without opening my eyes.

24. For the Light

For the light the sun lavishes on the dreary day
we thank the sun for its immeasurable sheet of light

for the night that falls to relieve the worker of fatigue
we thank the night for the vital supplies that keep us going

for the *ichabo* who steady the king infallible on the throne
we thank the loyal chiefs for providing the sovereign's support

for the evergreens that do not fall and clothe all seasons
we thank the faithful evergreens for the perennial cover

for the roots that hold us to the earth to thrust into the air
we thank the roots for the down-to-earth duty

for the voluminous basins the tributaries pour into the Niger
we thank the tributaries for supplying the great river's needs

for the clouds that shield us from cosmic missiles
we thank the clouds for blunting the brazen mortal glare

for the rain that falls to wet the land from scorching
we thank the rains for routing drought from the delta

for the cast-iron bell that completes the minstrel's costume
we thank the cast-iron bell that adequately equips the minstrel

for the mystery that keeps us fortunate and alive
we celebrate the mystery of the life we now live

for the muse that vigilantly gives the cue to the minstrel
we thank the muse for selflessly promoting another

for without direction signs my road maker installed all the way
I, the compulsive traveler, would have taken a wayward course.

25. Since You Entered

Since you entered
my riverboat of songs

it dances on the current
sailing itself into wider waters

to the music of Mami Wata's
ensemble of water maids

that drown the efforts of sirens
out there to cause a wreck.

Since you entered
my riverboat of songs

it's been so possessed
by currents of insistent drums

that we don't turn back
but gaze only at unending waters

from where the breeze whispers
to our ears blunting sirens

that will not give up
even after we broke their spell.

Since you entered
my riverboat of songs

the vast horizon beyond
beckons to the rites of ecstasy:

we are fishers of tunes
that we catch at every moment

that bears us to the river's
embrace of vast waters

in the union we seek
one body dissolving into the other.

Since you entered
my riverboat of songs

the sirens do not give up
their distractive spectacle

launching their breasts at
the boat that defies seduction

and our riverboat dances on
with the assurance of a charmed life

propelled by a force so infinite
and deep beyond comprehension

it breaks through the performance
that the sirens organize in ambush.

Since you entered
my riverboat of songs

the sirens still sing their hearts out
to draw the traveler out of his safe way

as they continue to stage hourly pageants
to blindfold the unwary and hold him hostage

but you are the sunbird among butterflies
and no semblance of colors and flight annuls the fact—

you subsume their superfluous antics
with the panache of the divine-endowed.

Since you entered
my riverboat of songs

diviners have become rich
preparing potions for seekers of love

merchants have more than tripled profits
selling dresses that do not hide dissemblers

pastors have quadrupled congregations
praying for the fantasies of faithless lovers.

Since you entered
my riverboat of songs

the Ethiope has become a sacred river
where pilgrims come to cleanse themselves

and make their vows
in exchange for divine grace.

Since you entered
my riverboat of songs

we have been so blessed
the riverboat glides effortlessly

accelerated by currents
in our body; a compulsive dance.

26. Bridal Song

The time has come
to renounce restraint

let go the crushing load
and swing around

what's life for
without a merry moment to relish?

Why belabor the body
with the task of titans

why walk the path of briars and thorns
when the paved avenue avails itself

why wear out the feet
when there's comfort in flight?

Give up the stone of a loaf
and tear away at the warm croissant

this is no time for bony tilapia
when there's abundance of *eban** to fill the palate

this is not the time to choose the hut
when a mansion opens its chambers to you

let go the cares of the world
and lift your favorite and dance *odjenema**

the divine powers have brought you to a fruiting plant
pluck your heart's content and enjoy the exhilarating juice

they have brought you to a spring
let your parched tongue fully revive its verve

the day has dawned, rise and seize the light
the sun looks down cheerfully, step from cold into warmth

hurray the potholed road is now smooth
speed up the drive to the tryst

take a sip of freshly tapped palm wine
share in rewards of patience come your way

let your smile smother memories of denial
have your fill of your life's desires

lay down the load you carry
saunter on to embrace the bride

put behind complaints put down anxieties
and give thanks for the newfound life

let go the crushing load
and swing around

behold the bride
share the joys of life

you have defeated rivals
revel at your victory

kiss your bride
kiss your bride.

* *eban*: to the traditional Urhobo, this is said to be the most
  delicious fish.
* *odjenema*: drums and dance of exhilaration.

27. I Stop by the Streamside

I stop by the streamside for inspiration
from the current murmuring to the waters;
the sing-song notes carry deep passion.

I observe the wind gently caressing leaves
to learn how to treat my partner properly;
in the crooning are gestures of intimacy.

I expose the full face to the sun's
early morning rays to learn to smile coolly
at my friend; love thrives on reciprocity.

I soak myself in the sunny and rainy melee,
the gods engrossed in their avid bacchanalia,
to be blessed with abundance; divine bonding.

I cherish dawn and dusk, foreplay for deeper experience
of respective day and night, to gain knowledge
of the right mood; even spontaneity needs preliminaries.

I seek the dewdrop's overlaying of leaves and grass
cooling the acute fever caused by the day's heat;
it is by covering the other that a couple survives hardship.

I see birds stick out their beaks
into the other's mouth in a solemn rite;
sharing without condition is a tenet of love.

I learn from around me the natural experience
of love in the flow, dialogue, reciprocal touches
that tell the human narrative of muse and minstrel.

28. Now That Their Smile is Infinite

Now that their smile is infinite with warmth
their steps bearing the assurance of adepts

the rites have the facility of discoverers
beating new paths into the heart of a new world

now that they dream in waking and wake to dream
they stand taller than the red woods of California

now that they speak with each other in their blood
their hearts beat a mystic rhythm of a mountain river

now that absence and presence belong to one nation
they have struck a new coin to celebrate sovereignty

now that their currency trades a high human value
and they uphold the pride of their dear land

now that the hen awakens the cockerel to crow
and he skirts round her with a flaring cockscomb

the cultic dance enters a crescendo
and no more can the music be contained in the heart

now that the gods have possessed their devotees
their movement is an effortless rhythm of faith

now that their new world is mapped out and shared
the resident sovereigns sit in their respective thrones

and look around with exhilaration at their dominion
and marvel at the infinite empire of contentment

they have built after crossing seven rivers
and conquering fear of drowning in depths

now they smile broadly at themselves
their graceful steps so assured and gingerly.

29. You Are the Sun

You are the sun that cheers up the day
that's become temperate since my coming out,

the wind to which the *eyareya* grass must bow;
the call that tugs at the heartstrings of the distant traveler.

You are the insistent memory
of everything dear at home that follows overseas:

the mountain that grows more picturesque
into a landmark that's the background to every vision

that the exile can no longer live peacefully without;
the tasteful water and refreshing air left behind

and only a return will allow to devour in abundance
and touch the *isene*-dappled* body of his abandoned bride,

inhale the singular *ugboduma** body odor
whose freshness smacks with tenderness,

taste the table salt of his nativity
and eat the dish that fills with desire for no other food.

With you there the raised flag of my sovereignty,
how independent am I without the old anthem?

With the priest exiled from his benevolent but jealous goddess,
what prayerful faith elsewhere in the world can bring him prosperity?

With you at home firmly held back by distance,
how can permanent residence for me outside be a refuge?

With you ever beckoning every breathing moment,
how can I defy the vision of salvation and have peace?

The traveler so far away from his heart's desire
prepares for a return to a nuptial feast,

defies all perils to fly back to be swathed
in the *owena*-embroidered* blanket of his heritage.

* *isene*: Urhobo word for cam wood dye.
* *ugboduma*: sweet-smelling leaf.
* *owena*: master artist in Urhobo/Edo tradition.

30. The Sirens' Assault

The day you were silent,
down with malarial fever,

that was the day nine sirens chose
to put on a spectacular pageant.

It was a rehearsed ambush
executed to the letter of a grand design.

The day the queen traveled out of town,
a livery of attendants vied for her throne;

the day the bride stepped out,
the maids stampeded to occupy her chamber—

they came one after the other, nine
groomed in different habits and perfumes;

their eyes fiery with charms
to strike whoever looked at them

and they launched their bodies
to highlight their obsession;

their tongues wearing a mellifluous gloss
so that they could have an easy catch with their baits.

They spiced their songs with delirium
to satiate whoever heard their voices,

they called from all cardinal points
to hide a concerted effort to break my fort;

adept in their craft like an army
they opened so many fronts in one battle.

Nine sirens singing their hearts sore,
they expected me to break away from you

to embrace them in their foxholes
and fall asleep in their bosoms.

First they afflicted you with fever
to have a free passage to me;

their intelligence was precise, but you
ever alert, hurled your body over them to cover me—

those your legs, lit large eyes, and full chest,
who can withstand them among the flatfooted?

They thought since I was alone
and you were down and far away,

they could knock me out
with one assault or another

but they knew not wherever we were
we lived together body and shadow.

They thought the thunder they bore
would bring down even the iroko

but whatever charm they acquired
from the shamans they consulted

you could counter, you medicine-woman;
healer extraordinary

whose partner nobody can strike down,
whose company protects from perils

and invoking your name just once
more than enough to knock out the army

to retreat posthaste
and hide in their desolate quarters.

Your vision before me
more than routed the would-be robbers

and above all your unfathomable care
more than shielded your minstrel

to serenade you, muse,
with this heartwarming song.

31. You Tell Me

You tell me
you have reset your clock

pushing it six hours backwards
from Nigerian to Eastern Standard Time;

you tell me
you reset your body clock to mine

so that we both live
in the same time zone

of one picturesque dawn
following a night of dreams

in one craft in one stream
borne by gleeful currents.

I have reset my clock
to tell the same time as yours

pushing forward six hours
from Eastern Standard to Nigerian Time

so that we both live
in the same time zone

of one picturesque dawn
following a night of dreams

in one craft in one stream
borne by gleeful currents.

You open your day to me
as I do mine to you—

I follow you from here
bedtime to work and back

as you do my every minute and step
nudging me in my tasks

and in the dream we share intertwined
in city parks and ocean beaches.

We share the same season
despite the latitudes apart:

when I am numb with blustery cold,
you stoke my fireplace with your hands

as when you are shivering all over
I do yours with more than my hands

from the malady that seizes
both of us in lonely spasms

and you set your sprinklers on
in my heat as I do in yours.

We share one body time
after resetting our clocks

but our world differs in time
and seasons from those of others

who know not the nuisance
they cause in reaching out to us

and disrupting the body time
we keep from their view.

32. A Walk in the Rain

I walk in the early morning rain
to keep pace with my partner

whom nobody sees in a sweatshirt
with a baseball cap covering her hair.

My wandering will be weird
to those who will never know

how it burns deep in the heart
to stay indoors fretting to no end.

Those whose deities are tame
and are not possessed by their faith

stay immoveable all daylong
and brag about the stone virtue

that keeps them in line
without straying a moment.

But there's no fire in them
to drive them into the open—

shelter is not a roof above the head,
nor keeping out of rain when there's fire.

I walk in the rain, drenched all over,
my deified one of course not wet;

two figures following the same
road signs to one destination.

The heavenly sprinklers are having
an effect on the company of the muse—

the forecast is of abundant sunshine,
which we are gingerly moving into.

33. For Saying "Thank You"

For saying "Thank you"
for doing my duty

for ignoring all other calls
to avail yourself to mine

for placing me on a pedestal
to tower above all others

for calling my name
with such musical finesse

for the singular honor
of hosting me in your heart

for taking so much care
of what I forget to do for myself

for the freedom
of reaching the other at will

for the gratitude
of the bird in the air

for the trust
in sharing the other's dream

for the destiny of the sun
to shower warm rays on the world

for coloring every breathing hour
with your magic brush of smiles

for the miracle of timely appearance
whenever I come across a depressing monster

for the grace of providing the cue
to the endless song on my lips

I have the liberty to say
"I love you."

34. Two Probing the Contours

Two probing the contours
of a newly discovered country

no day without a brighter gem
adding luster to the new world

no day without finding an unknown
to double the wonders of the discovery

no day without naming an unnamed
to make familiar an increasing population

no day without inhaling fresh fragrances
no day without touching more lives

no day without novel notes to acquire
no day without polyrhythm in the air

no day without the vocabulary expanding
to adopt words that tease our desires

no day without the tongue dialoguing freely
and opening doors to hidden treasures

no day without the sunny disposition
that makes a contented country

no day without birds playing in the open
brandishing their plumes with pride

no day without casting the spell
to make pets of wild creatures on the loose

no day without expanding horizons
with thoughts coasting beyond skylines

no day the blood is not a turbulent river
racing to seek solace in a union with the sea

no day the heart is not a bubbling spring
that restores the body with its healing power

no day we are not permanent residents
writing the constitution of a newly independent nation

no day we do not probe the contours
of the new territory expanding into its own universe

every day the terrain is so crowded with delight
every day only two savor the semi-divine treat.

35. I Hear Your Penetrating Call

I hear your penetrating call
and begin to gather my movables for a home return.
The hunter goes into the wilds,
his head filled with prancing deer and porcupine
but must return with or without the dream game.
I don't believe there's anything in the wilderness
that warrants leaving you alone at home.

I hear your penetrating call
and begin to gather my tools and harvest for a home return.
The farmer at the end of the day yearns
to return to the comfort of his home—
home is where you are, waiting; home
cannot be moved away to wherever you wander
but remains homely even with cracked walls and doors.

I hear your penetrating call
and begin to gather my movables for a home return.
Distance tortures me with a plethora of denials
and only a return assures of a solution to the crisis.
I cannot spend more time in the thorn bush
while a down-laden bed always awaits me.
I want us to hold hands and laugh together.

I hear your penetrating call
and begin to return to the divine gift
awaiting me in the very home I fled;
there's none here that's comparable
to the beauty you carry and keep at home.
I am on my way to you, on the way
to the queen that assures me of kingship.

I hear your penetrating call
in my heart already beating a triumphant return
to the joy that makes home the place to be
because you are there and I am coming to you
and because life away is an unending torture
and only returning to embrace you is the cure.
Of course, you are the remedy to nightmares away.

36. I Paint You

I paint you with colors from my heart:
radiant with rays of the rising sun
(your head wears a semi-divine wrap).
I paint you with warm colors because
you shower rainbow smiles to arrest every eye
and the world holds you so high up in the sky
above the bevy of birds whose plumes
define beauty in supernatural flights of shades.

I paint you radiant wearing a fiery crown,
enthroned queen in a happy kingdom.
I paint you with cam wood colors
since you are the bride extraordinary
in the ageless beauty that befits a deity.
I paint you with palm kernel's golden oil
to soften to a shine your lucent skin.
Ubiebi fude! Darkness that glows!

I paint you with a brush of strokes
from an inexhaustible pool of colors
because you possess every article of beauty.
I paint your portrait with the craft
of Owena, assured of all the years of practice
and with the elegance of my Benin heritage.

Your coiffure tinted with red petals,
neck laced with corals befitting a princess;
you have wrapped yourself to the chest
with the white of Olokun's livery
and an escort of leather fans and ivory horns
serenade you from the repertory of praise chants.

Bride of all times, beauty that astounds
with the radiance of the full moon,
what artist has the superhuman craft
to do justice to the charm of your figure
with a lamp infinitely fuelled from inside?
I'll exhaust all warm and cool colors
and still fall short of your brilliance
and so end up casting you in bronze.

37. I Will Wait Out

I will wait out the croc's legendary patience
for thickening clouds to leave a face of sunny smiles

I will break the unbreakable record
for what I hold dear in the heart

I must damn the waiting-for-Godot cynics
for the appearance of dawn however long the night

I won't be blinded to retreat
but wade through streams of mud to diamond

I won't mind the amount of stupendous sacrifice
to build an everlasting monument

I am ready to bear graphic bruises
fighting to rescue my bartered bride from brigands

the river crashes from the mountain's top into the sea
to have its desired union

the squirrel in a fit of hunger
cracks the palm kernel with its teeth for survival

I must wait limping months for the one
whose presence completes my company

I must wait weak-kneed weeks for the only one
who more than suffices out of an uncountable number.

I will wait the longest day to enter the space
that rounds off my circle

I will break the unbreakable record
for what I hold dear in the heart.

38. I Abandon Chores

I abandon the countless chores crying for attention
and enthralled by your music follow the strange spirit

to where the rhythm leads to a dance
that stirs mind and body into a trance.

Take me to where the current flows,
carry me through diverse terrains to wider waters

and let me experience the special drafts ahead
for I stifle in the imposed confinement here.

I see birds fly yonder singing choruses
that lift my heart with them into the clouds;

I want to be where strangers live out their fantasies
beyond yearnings of those languishing in institutions.

My thoughts fly to the mountain ranges
that challenge pedestrian movement

to behold the spectacular heights out there;
the peak that is attainable without fuss,

and there distant perch at the crossroads
before lifting to the congress of happy spirits—

what the gods wish for themselves
but cannot have because not human.

Tell me I am distracted and I'll laugh you off
as a fool who knows not romance is a trance

like gulping wine without knowing its crazy spirit,
throwing about flames in a thatched home without fear

and I follow the vagabond spirit lost in the music;
a drowned man in the open arms of the water queen.

39. I Am Looking for a Cure

I am looking for a cure for a malady
whose only cure may be more of the malady itself—

the doctor can open up the heart in a theatre
but won't find tissues of the body-racking ache to remove;

the diviner can tell the crazy end the symptoms lead to
but no craft to forestall the inevitable with cowries and herbs.

Some folks will go to the extent of cursing their fates
for not suffering from the psychedelic malady;

others will wade and drown in tears for always running foul
of luck on whom to partner with to suffer the malady.

Whether they suffer from the malady and are pained
or are pained because of not falling into a delirium,

they won't have peace at night or day
and yearn to be struck by the malady.

When struck, some patients migrate to the moon
and there strip themselves of rational habits

and worship moon rocks in the name of their faith
or in naked splendor shower in the full moon's blaze.

Others set sail to undiscovered islands
to live in paradise without dying

or get their share of heaven and leave
the rest of their lives to a hedonist's dream.

And yet others go into exile in their homelands
and dance in the rain without ever getting wet.

And so those who are struck are mad in every way;
those passed by what others call a malady are mad

hence the cure is more of the malady the malady the cure;
the same fates for those struck and those spared!

40. My Beloved Sent Word

My beloved sent word to me
to come without delay.
I am going immediately.
I can't count my blessings with her.

Nowhere is too distant
        to answer her call from.
No road is too rough
        to travel when she calls.
I am so financially strapped
but no time is too hard
        not to heed her call.
I will borrow to accomplish my needs
and work hard to pay back the loan.
I can never be too fatigued
        not to answer her call.
Neither thick night nor thundering storm
        will hold me down.
I am on my way,
I will go straight there.

My beloved sent word to me
to come without delay.
I am going immediately.
Through the farthest distance
the worst of roads
the harshest of times
aching fatigue
thickest night or thundering storm
I am going to her
and wish I can pay back for her many blessings.

41. As the Chant Rises

As the chant rises in its last turn
and veers into the bridal chamber

the cockerel flares his cockscomb
in the penultimate rite of manhood

the partner pants from a flash of fever
that has thrown the tryst into a delirium

the drums beat themselves into a crescendo
that carries along trembling leaves of the forest

and all bowing to the divine spirit
that leads the livery into a final assault

to break the erstwhile impregnable gate
and take in the vagrant knight to a restful lodge.

The creeks have sated themselves with draughts
the sea battling to liberate the waves

that have been conscripted to scare off
the boat from berthing in a destined haven

the constricted passage swept open by breeze
lo the dance smacks the body with sweat

one more swing and the world's a burst of fireflies
one more pitch that lifts the body to the stars

the python guard leaves its post
Mami Wata waits restless for her consort

the dancers are falling into a swirl of music
the march melts into a possessed shout

we are not done with the frenzied forest flares
only done with a flourish falling into silence

with fire and water at peace, dawn's breeze
fanning the earth's body with a cooling glow.

42. The Wind Blows

The wind blows with its seasonal ardor,
and along its way every tall grass bows;

the sun brags with its familiar brazen strut
with the world adapting to blunt its stern gaze

but all of a sudden an eternity shrinks
into a matter of days on the horizon;

the last stretch of a once-unending road,
a mountain melting away into a plain

only around the corner that annuls distance
and makes victory over time a consistent stride.

Without effort I see beyond the hill
that has grown between us over the months.

Am I taller than when we last met
or have I scaled through the peak?

The hill must be melting by the hour;
it is warming up at an alarming rate!

Or are you growing taller where you stand
to now give me so much unhindered vision?

It's only upon arrival we'll check our heights,
after the hill has been consumed by the fire in our hearts.

43. His Song Gathered Timbre

His song gathered timbre
from the storm that blew in his body—

in eight days the moon will shine fully
on two plowing a field of magic crops;

in a short while the sky's broad face
will be mobbed by smiles in all directions.

Over the stretch, at the corner
the march enters its final hurrah—

where two friendly forces meet in a battle,
the field turns into one body, one formation;

the exile at the last landmark on the way home
kneels before it to absorb memories of old

that will spice the new life he expects in the home
he freshly fashions out of multiple memories

of what it has been outside that drew him away
and the enduring legacy that he returns to for paradise.

44. The Cry of the Water-Bird

The cry of the water-bird tears the heart—
it's not the song I expect from free ones.

Looking at the beauty of her plumage, who will
not envy her spread on water and then in the air?

Looking at her breasts, who will not relish
brushing her and serenading beauty of the blessed,

since her wings lift her beyond the pedestrian walk
free to strut, swim, and fly and live where she wants?

But in the bird, a woman emerges from the mask
to contend with domination and dependency;

her lord hones the craft of conditioning her
to fear freedom; her own whiplashing censor.

❋   ❋   ❋

How does the minstrel
distil his muse's tears?

A long stream of sighs
so painful over decades

when possessed, not in a delirium
but of a patriarch's chattel slavery

waiting, a vessel whose properties
sate the hunger to assuage age—

the bird-woman waits there; he comes
to get draughts from one of many waterholes

and cares not if she knows joy in her veins
if the fire burning her is doused with rain.

I know the current rage, starved for months; not
given her due, the bird that cries rather than sings,

conditioned from the real bird she is
to a benumbed woman; a broken slave.

I know your pain, I wipe your tears
and install you my muse, keeper of fire

and whose fever I share totally,
basking in the kindling warmth.

45. We Read the Book of Dreams

We read the book of dreams
in our wakeful hours, hence

my pigeon breaks out of a cage for fresh corn
and performs magic to chase me out of diurnal grind;

we survive on an oasis of milk
and sing a song of contentment in a desert country.

Because we read the book of dreams
five days turn into cowries in a bowl

and we pick one out at a time
in anticipation of the great festival ahead.

We are preparing a nest in the clouds
where with abandon birds can live birdly lives.

The book of dreams always opens
borders we can cross without passports;

it opens to playgrounds
that turn us into children.

The book of dreams denies no favors;
we get what we seek from fruiting trees,

have swimming pools in our backyard
and beaches where waves kiss our bare feet

for we are the fortunate lovers
given a chance to catch stars as sea shells.

We read the book of dreams, dream our lives
and now we are happy aliens in a restricted land.

Together we read the book of dreams
in which five days to the tryst is a mountain

we scale through with wings of fugitive birds;
a sea we cross without fear of water or drowning.

46. Four is Not a Random Number

Four is not a random number in rituals;
so four days ahead carry their own import.

Every four days the market convenes
and between those numbers of only four

spirits consort with humans, dead and living;
all out to prepare the ground for trading,

the day of exchange, barter, getting needs
or the pleasantries that give life contentment.

In four days the congress convenes
for lovers to meet and range freely

under cover of a capital crowd
that guarantees anticipated freedom.

Four days is not a random number in rituals;
one stop after another and then another

and in four days solemnize the journey
of two as one; four days one leap ahead.

47. Wounds However Deep Heal

Wounds however deep heal with medication,
care, and time and so have your savage ones.

Now the scars are sad reminders of
broken wings, iron cage, and starvation

but coasting in the clouds, who still feels
the pain of decades, confinement and torture?

Even now many see the scars as beauty spots;
no longer reminders of torture and splotches.

Now every horizon opens up and taunts
with fresh discovery of gardens whose

special flowers, fountains, and sheer
fresh air give zest to flying heavenly high

and only now can the bird really exercise
the dividends of divine-proffered freedom.

This delight is even more ecstatic because
the wounds have healed, the scars gone

with the indescribable paradise that's
life of abundance that was once denied.

Wounds however deep heal with medication,
care, and time and so have your savage ones.

48. The Fruiting Tree

When the fruiting otie *tree* sees its favorite,*
it gladly showers on him its ripest fruits.

It's as the groom feels one day is
too long away to meet his bride

after an eternity has disappeared
into a matter of twenty-four hours

and the entry will not be accompanied
by cannons but slipping in at dusk

under cover of a harmattan haze
that swathes all in a cool brown linen

to be welcomed by a sole witness
stealing in to hear the minstrel's serenade

and he knows she is the sole witness
to his homecoming amidst a throng.

When the fruiting otie *tree sees its favorite,*
it gladly showers on him its ripest fruits.

---

* otie: the Urhobo for the cherry-fruit tree, which is said to
shower fruits down at the arrival of its favorites.

49. Sun and Moon in Mock Battle

And on the day the sun and the moon in mock combat,
the gods display their crafts to the other's applause

the world would fall from its orbit if it hung on slender tethers
the earth would sink into emptiness if it was not full of itself

the waters would swallow the rest of the universe wholesale
if the power of others does not surpass the force of oceans

the air would stifle all the living and leave them to die
if it did not depend on others for its own existence and survival

and the vast world shrank into one body
the entire universe was only one room.

Even if titans tested temerity on the approval of others,
they would still be saddled with immeasurable delight

and there's no end to what memories will bring to songs
that will outlive the moment, outlive the celebrants

covered with vines whose leaves and flowers
enchant them with the pleasures of paradise

and whoever sings the song henceforth
should sing alleluia to affirm faith in the other

for the fact remains that in a world of so many
only one more than suffices when it comes to the test

and when the *otie* plant sees its favorites,
it gladly showers on them its ripest fruits

and now the tale will be told without knowledge
of the distance and years that brought about

the congress of stars at the beach, the effulgence
of complementing ones outshining themselves

and remain in the shadows of the wide world,
contented with the fortune of muse and minstrel.

50. Love in a Time of Grief and Strife

I

The day lightning struck the *uwara* in Lagos at midlife
the same day a thunderstorm drowned an entire town

the young beauty that was every neighbor's favorite
fell off the cliff in thunder and left unprecedented deluge

the community has its totem slaughtered in the abattoir
and peace transforms into a mauling monster in the streets

the river that has nowhere else to divert its floodwaters
starts a tearful event for everyone on its swollen course—

the falling of the uwara at midlife however far away
has spread high fever to Delta folks and water spirits

the harmattan brushfire consuming Jos and its environs flares
nerves across the nation blowing hot and cold at the same time

the day the muse wept blood, the minstrel gasped at a bloodbath
the day that held the key to celebration the same day blackened

the same fire in the heart razing humans in wrong quarters;
individual wails and communal tears for one death too many

for a withering mother as for a best friend; one blood spill subsumes
the peace of a dream city and ushers in a nightmarish chapter

when there's no place for the sunflower to bloom in a cosmic rage,
the community sets up roadblocks to hunt down the innocent
    as game

the news from LUTH* of a patient dying needlessly
with no doctors to attend to her in a whole day

runs parallel to JUTH* in a tin city with an army division
and the Nigerian Army dissolved into bloody sectarians

the same casualties of incompetence, an entire community
cleansed out of their rocky homes by high-powered arsonists

the muse weeps for her broken heart and deep wounds
the minstrel rails against injustice and the butchery of peace.

II
Love continues to flourish at a time of strife
as at a time of grief. Neither fracturing

in the blood-tinted theatre of combatants
nor the benumbing wails of sudden loss

can tear apart the warm spirit that binds hearts
and brings two into one doting on the other.

In a time of bloody strife and of sudden grief,
love heals the deep bruises that tear others apart

and I sing to the muse who stirs my heart to bleed
a stream of songs as I long to hold her to my chest.

* LUTH: Lagos University Teaching Hospital.
* JUTH: Jos University Teaching Hospital.

51. If You Were to Kill Me

If you were to kill me, the mystery
would remain unsolved—no fingerprints

from pawing about your body, lips,
breasts, and armpits I love to tickle

for the CID* to match to you the real person;
no scent for police dogs to lead to your heart

that possessed me into a tumultuous frenzy
to be unmindful of excesses of habits.

And that won't be all—no postmortem to examine
my heart whose aorta you savagely broke

from center to the sides, a River Niger
at flood time but of gushing blood

and it bled for days I cried to you
to stop the hemorrhage of vital fluids

to rescue me from the wound you inflicted;
the fire you stoke and leave burning wild.

Nobody will link you to the gruesome act
though loving you has been a terrible malady—

remember you described it as such
and I know it because I suffer it—

its onset brought unspeakable fever
and insomniac nights in which I pined away

singing madly to myself of one whose love
more than exceeds an emperor's for Cleopatra

but while your switched-off phones
made you sleep soundly over the emergency

and the wild fire burned inside me without smoke
the heart lacerated as by a keen knife

all contributing to my demise
you started as a forest fire arsonist

safe in bed not even knowing the anguish
of it all; the burning and profuse bleeding

that condemned me, you away,
to the pain that hands one over to death.

If I were to die because of you,
loving you to a severe malady

no-one will trace you to the incident;
neither fingerprints nor scent available

and as for the DNA, the police will conclude
that minstrelsy is a self-killing profession

without telling the world of the muse's
drowning me in a delirium and walking away

as I came down in unspeakable pain;
martyred proclaiming faith in your heart.

* CID: Nigeria's Criminal Investigation Department,
  now with a new name.

52. When You Are Silent

When you are silent and incommunicado
why do I imagine doomsday breaking upon the earth

when I don't hear from you in a matter of only twenty-four hours
why does my mind run into abysmal missteps or tripping

when you don't phone or text me when I expect you to
why do I prepare to wear sackcloth

why do I dream of you as an alien from a still undiscovered country
why do I envision you suffering from a malady not in the
    medical manual

do I know that you need a room of your own to muse, inhale
    and exhale
do I know you need to be alone to explore the vast landscape
    within you

do I give you enough space to practice your self-affirming rituals
without flashing the sun at you to let you be yourself for once

why do I hold my breath like the mother of an only child
when I cannot reach you immediately whenever I want

why do I drive you every absent moment on a rocky mountain
    precipice
where wild winds from nowhere can blow you into deep damnation

why do I eternal optimist suffer insomnia and heartaches
when you go to bed in a complete lockdown of phones and worries

why do the demons of absence assault me so savagely
and dump me in a wilderness to find my way out into safety

why do mischievous djinns close your mouth a divine organ
they know will break into song and heal my lacerated heart

when you are silent and incommunicado
why do I imagine a mob neck-lacing you

when you take your time to wake and be available
why do I imagine you running into armed robbers

why not imagine you going into a belated fattening room
to learn the mysteries of opening a man's heart without hurt

why not imagine you hibernating a bird in an exile season
preening your feathers to flutter to the stir of my eyes

why not imagine you daydreaming walking me to an altar
why not dreaming of eloping with you to settle in a full moon

don't you need to be alone to calm the whirlwinds raging in you
don't you need to cool the body burning without flame or smoke

do I know you are a sovereign though in alliance with me
why do I palpitate when you are my muse and I your minstrel?

You must forgive me for running you into ravines and kidnappers;
you must forgive me for singling you out for nightmares.

53. Aftermath

I
You are the caravan of my dreams;
you take me to the oasis of the desert.

With your constant presence, I'm lost
to the world but sure of my direction;

you make the road I travel,
you lead the way to my destination

where a fountain pours at all times
the seasons unfailing in their drafts

in songs that make meaning to love,
partnership through distant terrains.

Did we seek the meeting by chance
or was it a command from above

to bring together medicine-woman
and patient, queen and king of hearts?

You are the caravan of my dreams,
the spirit that leads me to and from

the pilgrimage so out of the way that
without you I would be totally lost

but you are the caravan of my dreams;
you take me to the oasis of the desert.

II
Our caravan weighed down
by such wealth of gems and spices

how do we leave the oasis
without a song of satiation on our lips

where do we go in the pilgrimage
after garnering divine blessings

what have other sacred sites to offer
after the canonization of the living

the beauty we have seen in its resplendence
how relate to the vulgar world

without drawing the envy of lovers
or the wrath of those who can't dream?

We witnessed the wonder, we came out
of the deluge of cornucopia, a delirium

that no other beauty seeks to excel;
the beauty memory celebrates daily

bringing you and me to the same tent,
the same hour in a caravan of contentment.

III
Now that the rites of ecstasy are performed
entered the exclusive Cloud 9 for a divine treat

now muse and minstrel have started a new life
the landscape within changed to a picturesque postcard

the echoes from the bridal chamber ring of laughter,
the bed a nest of contented birds in the sun.

When we live every minute of the dream,
memory becomes a streak of fireworks;

the blazing full moon subsumes all other lights
one expects nothing more from faces lucent with joy.

54. We Live in a Full Moon

We live in a full moon
relishing the roundness of its ripe fruit

the full moon is a ball of fire
whose flames deck the entire sky

oftentimes it is golden with delight
at other times red or blue but ever bright

the full moon blazes in the heart
the heart is aflame with full moonlight

we live in a full moon
two figures nobody knows

their profiles metamorphose into
planetary partners of diverse roles

new myths begin in hiding safely
in the full moonlight glare

a full moon for a round fruit
we desire to fill the heart's hunger

faces glow with contentment
with a roundness of the full moon

the cosmic fruit a ball of fire
the sky's supreme makeup

there's a full moon blazing
across the breadth of the heart

we play hide-and-seek in moonlight
call and respond in the full moon

we tell folktales of birds and animals
in the full moon that blazes in our hearts

we sing arcane songs of love
the moon has delivered to us

the full moon kindles the fires
that already burn bright in us

we live in a full moon
whose provocation we enjoy

by abandoning whatever chores
and going outside to live in its blaze.

55. Butterflies in My Heart

All species of butterflies assemble in my heart
for a beauty pageant that will go into the record

o heart, flutter to the pageantry of arresting colors
relish the festival air that blows all over

the birds are calling and responding with songs
that resonate in the inner chamber of my heart

the polyrhythmic music rocking my heart
to dance energetically will go into the record

o heart, hold with all your muscles the beautiful muse
a goddess of a kind whose song possesses you

a blazing rainbow arches the breadth of my heart
for a spectacle that will go into the record

o heart, assemble the spirit flutists the muse provides
and dance gracefully to the music of their repertory

I am at heart not just Tanure everybody knows
I am an exile in a faraway country of freedom

my heart tends a garden blooming with sunflowers
dispersing a fragrance so exotic it will go into the record

it is my heart that celebrates this beauty in its open spaces
with butterflies, birds, rainbow, and flowers all over

I celebrate my heart not on rooftops but in the blind spot
of ventricles a euphoria that will surely go into the record

for the muse's divine love my blessing and no end
to serenading this beauty that will go into the record.

56. On This Valentine's Day

I take your self-brewed wine
from your carefully kept chalice

as you chant me songs of manhood,
cheer me on to destroy demons of doubt

that litter the land we call homeland
prowling to sour the sweetness ahead of us.

I am drunk with passion for you,
respond to your call to eliminate every doubt—

there's a new dream that belies the past;
there's a new presence that's paramount.

I drink this wine from the chalice
you offer me as a welcoming toast,

invoke not Bacchus but our own Aridon
to proffer me a befitting gift to my favorite,

to always thrust me beside you
your knight every moment of the day.

I carry you in my bloodstream so that always
you reside deep in every cell of my body;

we have to be lamps competing in brightness
to discover the other's hidden treasures.

I take your self-brewed wine so strong
from the carefully kept chalice of your being

knowing your invaluable gift as
coming straight from my eternal dream;

my long dream of ages has turned
into the eternal gift of your quest.

I drink heartily the wine from the chalice
you present to me as a welcoming toast;

you are the invisible muse behind my music,
medicine-woman and magician emboldening my every move;

whoever hears this song should remember
the remote sources of the Niger and Ethiope Rivers,

whoever's arrested by my voice should remember
the palm-wine that's distilled into potent savory gin.

I take wine from the special chalice
you offer me the fortunate one as a toast;

you are the rock from which the legendary spring
derives its purity, freshness, and flavor;

without you the spring will be so exposed it will
be polluted and without its trademark selling points.

With your wine there's no blood in my wound,
no hurt in bruises only gumption to live happily;

invoking you accelerates the road to my destination,
my desire for you waxes into a cheerful full moon;

only you medicine-woman and magician know the cure
for the malady you also suffer from that knocks me out.

I drink this wine from the specially kept chalice
you fill to the brim with all your resources;

"I'm not experienced at brewing," you say
but your vintage excels the products of professionals.

I drink your self-brewed wine so strong
from the carefully kept chalice of your body

that you offer me as a welcome toast
on this Valentine's Day.

57. After

After the hallucination of the divine communion
how can we separate the muse from the minstrel

after the trance in a transcendental nest for the two
how will the birds live normal lives among their kind

after the self-immersion in the other and total absorption
how can one alone be whole without the other now part

after the colorful installation in a radiant throne of gold
how are you queen and I not king of the same dominion

after the flight across oceans of mountainous clouds
why should separate nests and not one big one hold us

after going through rites of pain and now exhilaration
why will priest and priestess not submit to their deity

after discovering we suffer from the same malady
why will we not seek a cure even if it's more of the malady

after the declaration of independence after a hard-fought war
why should we not plant a sovereign flag in our territory

after a victory drum begins to beat in our body
why will we not dance to the primordial rhythms

after crossing the seven rivers to the haunted forest
how will we not create a bonfire with wood that burns so bright

after so many days and months in the journey
how will we not carry memories like a badge of honor

and after the beauty we have seen together in our wanderings
how will others understand our outlandish habits and songs?

58. Full Cycle

I

Now you more than fill the very cup and gulp draughts of
what you once considered unacceptable; a complete retreat.

You, priestess of sharing for peace's sake, were once
too ready to give up your favorite possession to be split

into two, three, four, or more than five quarters
that barely left you a modicum of your body's desire;

you were content with so little to avoid rancor you didn't
want to shatter the peace you revered above everything else.

You accepted whatever morsel and never lunged at the whole;
you didn't want to confront riots against a gluttonous mandate

that afflicted others so much as to drive them crazy
and take to violence and malice to hold their own,

and that meant protecting theirs by arms and contrivance.
Once the priestess of peace and unruffled when cheated,

you waited serenely for whatever is left for you; but no more
can you wait and scramble in the open race for your desire;

no more do you want anything but the whole, the entire
onto your insatiable self; enough of unfulfilling nights;

a hawk of steeled talons to snatch and devour your catch.
You no longer shut yourself in and care less if you stir a rabble.

You were once a celebrated priestess of peace, ready
to be taunted with a crumb of a pumpkin or even starve;

you once smiled over rioting desires as a destitute army assaulting
the body; you stepped aside for poachers to take over your domain,

but no more. You have become a glutton seeking satiation
with missionary zeal; quick to seek a fight to survive on all—

the honeycomb you do not want others to harvest with you
or the love gift you want others not touch with disrespect;

you now denounce priesthood of peace as apostasy of love
and promote fantasy to foster calm in your body polity.

Once you wouldn't mind a bit the season's rain
falling on the entire landscape however light

for every farmer however deserving to smile broadly
for contentment to be spread to whoever sought it,

but now you want only your crops to be so irrigated
as to enjoy a singular harvest no matter the cost to others.

A priestess of peace now costumed in war gear,
you will rout the legendary Amazons in the battlefield;

once a selfless sharer of bounty now a glutton,
you will shut others out of your blessing even in famine.

I see what the malady's fierce affliction has done to you
that more than fills the minstrel's voracious appetite

and I sing this song for your regained humanity
even as your divinity strikes me with such awe.

II
I started to feel the subtle transformation
from selfless sharer of pumpkin to glutton

in questions that startled and confused me: "What
of your Kano, Malaysian, and Amassoma friends?"

I had confessed to each location where
a woman had stepped out to offer me love gifts

before I met you and tripped in daylight
frittering away my night in daydreams.

I had humanized a goddess by naming her,
deified a woman whose path and mine met.

"I will show up very late at your end at night
and see how lonely like me you are there too!"

You have learned to set traps around me;
you show you really mean business in the hunt

and I can no longer be surprised at your behavior,
the malady we both suffer from without reprieve—

you are capable of setting detectives after me;
you are stalking my heart in an abstract mask.

"I won't allow you rest from my unrelenting gaze;
no more will I leave you alone, always beside you."

You tease and tickle me: calling yourself No. 19
in the fantasy harem you built for your minstrel;

you have so multiplied your non-existent rivals
because you can no longer share even with one.

But I remain unexpectedly calm in your storm,
for remove 9 and you are No. 1, my favorite!

59. Perhaps No Court Can Hear This

Perhaps no court can hear this
and pass judgment; only a mistrial

that whatever jury returns
will give the verdict of right and wrong.

I have heard the acquitted
confess to guilt in public

the guilty swear to innocence
that makes no sense.

Perhaps there's nowhere
to appeal to

even if condemned for fleeing
from a burning house into rain

or seeking refuge in a private house
in a devastating storm.

The public tongue
will always lash out

at vagabonds, loose ones
and throw dirt at others.

Perhaps neither rain nor fire
will open doors of reprieve

and I seek no acquittal
in my "Not guilty" plea.

60. What If

What if
the sky pours fish and frogs to drown the harmattan

what if
the perennial river dries up in a regular season

what if
our free hearts are besieged by fear

what if
our love song gets stuck to the throat

what if
the beautiful flower in our garden chokes from its fragrance

what if
our magic lute will not sing

what if
our refuge burns from a passerby's cigarette butt

what if
rumors smoke us out of the cloud cover

what if
our password is lost to our private needs

what if
the sun refuses to set in our day

what if
our memory erases vows solemnized with blood

what if
love strikes us with an improvised explosive device

what if
the muse burns the only copy of the minstrel's manuscript

what if
what if?

61. In Full View

I had planned for retirement as a safari
traveling to exotic places to capture live the picturesque

that neither the Travel Channel nor the *National Geographic*
could boast of to feed the frenzy of their insular clients.

Dreams have transported me so far away
to seek spotless beauties that are so out of this world

but only there not within practical means
and so can only come imagined or dreamed about—

after all what's dreamed about exists somewhere
in the world only if I traveled so far from the known world.

I thought I had got more than a fair share
of the spectacle that gladdens the conventional heart—

savannah gazelles grazing millet and sorghum farms;
forest antelopes playing hide and seek in arboreal shadows

and I am still haunted by the gaze of the graceful giraffe
that made the veldt a postcard of memory's pageants.

I couldn't catch the smudges of distant belles from this corner
and saw no local carrying the features of the beauty I desired.

Now I won't travel to the most dreamed-about places
for what's here that beats their best with divine elegance;

I no longer plan for a safari thousands of miles away
but will surely busy myself here relishing this discovery.

62. The Jury's Verdict: On Sunday

I am guilty: the jury's unanimous verdict.
They condemn me to a life sentence

with zero tolerance for break-ins
even if to let one out of bondage.

I would still be guilty even if I broke out
after being kidnapped into solitary confinement!

They would rather watch partners die
than revive their atrophied hearts to live happily;

they would rather return fugitive slaves
to torture than allow them entry into a free state,

they would rather push lovers on a precipice into
a ravine than reprieve the lost souls with understanding;

they would rather see the two raving mad create a spectacle
than quiet the storm blowing inside them to be normal;

they would rather watch the desert wanderers parch
to death than allow them a place in the waterhole.

None of them would douse the burning souls
with water; they know not the malady's agony.

The few who would glimpse the wildfire in the partners'
chests and know the rack they suffer were thrown out

to seat those tainted with Pentecostal piety
that everybody knows is a flimsy carapace;

the bold witnesses are struck deaf and dumb,
and nobody else can vouch I am not a vagabond.

I have only the supreme court of humanity
to judge the case and decide my fate

and my taciturn muse holds in her heart
the crucial evidence that would set me free.

63. If You Feel Your Partner's Hurt

If you feel your partner's hurt
deep in your bone's marrow

if you take in your favorite's blow
as an unrelenting hammer blow

if you feel your friend's chronic headache
as dealing you insomniac murmurs

if you experience your love's nightmare
as a haunting ogre

you already know what
you don't need to go to school for

that not to hurt yourself
is not to hurt another

hurting someone
inflicts hurt on you

to be hurt is
to hurt another

for we are not isolated
but bound as one

and what touches a part
touches one

and one cannot be whole
if the other is not

hence one's pain hurts the other
more than the afflicted.

64. I Exorcize

I exorcize the wandering evil spirit
by telling you about the two sirens

who the same hour bared their breasts
in a seductive dance to which they invited me.

I am expecting my favorite's dish still on the fire
and here comes one to taunt my appetite with a gruel!

I am priming my ears for the melody of my love's voice
and here steps in a pretender croaking without stop!

I am stepping forward to embrace my muse
and standing between us this prosaic phantom!

I do not want to keep a treasure in your breast
and be the thief to break in to steal it!

I will not pour arsenic into the very food
we share with so much zest;

I will never exchange the diamond I am
fortunate to possess for plastic beads or cowries . . .

Now that I have told you about the two sirens
who bared their breasts in a dance I declined to join,

I have no load to carry to slow me down;
I can spring to you and lift you in the air.

65. I Have Asked Myself

I have asked myself a thousand times
the troubling question, "Wetin man go do?"

I have prayed to push out the elephant
to occupy the room I couldn't fill with grace;

my victory following the Warri mantra*
often robs many others of their medals;

the god I pray to a partial deity
that closes ears to other worshipers.

Have I in manhood mustered guts
to host Ogidigbo's daughter*

without smudging her immaculate swath
with pawing overextended hands?

Beauty often sweeps me off my feet,
singing its praises even when sinister.

Have I not gone back on serene words
to reopen a closed path I need not pass?

"*You don fail me,*" I hear trailing me;
the voices of those above and below.

And I sing this song of the day
from the wrongs forgiven, harvest

the crop of nostalgic peace from
the silence of a threatening mob.

* Warri mantra: "*Wafi* man no dey carry last!" One has to
  succeed by all means.
* Ogidigbo's daughter: member of a traditional religious sect of
  beautiful women dedicated to a river god and always dressed in
  white to reflect their supposed purity. The sect is based in Kokori
  in Nigeria's Delta State.

66. I Want to Tell Everyone

I want to tell everyone I love you
but can't because it needs not be done—

there are things you can't admit to knowing
like someone always beside you but far elsewhere;

there's a dish you savor but whose cook is unknown—
how many times we don't know who to compliment?

I want to tell everyone I love you
but you can't be loved by the rules of the caste.

We know what's possible but impossible to others;
contentment is a ripe fruit hanging from the sky—

stand still and you miss it; fly and you snatch it;
there's no gravity love cannot defy with impunity.

I want to tell everyone I love you
but won't let the bull out of the lot;

I won't smear the moon with black smudges
nor bring down a deity to the mud to worship.

I want to tell everyone I love you,
everyone hearing my song but not my hurt;

because they drink enough in the drought
they know not the glass spilled so much.

I want to tell everyone I love you
but who cares to read my lips you bit?

If I tell everyone I love you
won't they set every nest ablaze for the residents' treason,

won't they replace gardens with a desert landscape
or cut down every tree of the forest to rid it of a hiding place?

I want to tell everyone I love you,
the moon is witness to the fire I bear in my heart.

I want the reed to dance ecstatically in the current,
water to fall from the mountain in a perennial flourish

I want to tell everyone I love you
as if they don't know I love you if I don't tell;

I want to tell everyone I love you
as if those who need to know don't already know!

67. When You Waited for My Call

You tell me you least expected that this far from girlhood,
self-proclaimed ripe, you could be so savaged by love thoughts

with invisible but keen lancets stabbing your breasts, heart, and more
to pain but not bleed, leaving you no moment to sleep but only
daydream.

And there you were struck silent but distracted all over,
you talking to no one and cooped in your bedroom darkened

by a listless spread you would never have thought of adopting;
you a stranger you were scared to stare at in the misted mirror.

I imagine you spread-eagled in bed by the melancholy of the malady
we wished ourselves now so real it is an unforgiving succubus;

I imagine you listening to the silent echoes of my voice,
your thoughts running amok seeking your fugitive magician

to talk to you in late hour moments not only serenading you
but also dishing you a hallucinating potion from deep lore—

you imagine him smothering you with the best of his spells, lifting
you beyond the peak of the Kilimanjaro; cresting beyond clouds.

You are the hen expecting a flaring cockscomb in a dance
without dawn—untiring foretaste of an exhilarating rite.

Knowing your glittering large eyes, your perennial luster
buoyant and bouncing, how could you look different

because your minstrel was held down from calling you
and not keeping to the ritual of lavishing you with songs?

Sorry for the pangs I caused you with the expected call
that didn't come; you waited afflicted by a slew of silence;

you suffered insomnia, fever, head and body aches
because you waited for my call that didn't come;

the only day you didn't shut down your phones
that was the day the call did not come all night.

Age provides no immunity to the heart's palpitations;
you know once the wind blows the wiregrass dances!

So even at your ripeness you are more vulnerable to fears
that you are being "posted" even when you are being missed;

at your fullness the malady exacts its highest price
and there's no faith as possessing as this storm within.

And so distant from girlhood, so womanly the more human
your needs more voluptuous than ever before in abundance.

So my muse let the magician minstrel send this song
to assuage the heart and assure you of a healing remedy.

68. In Contentment

In contentment the grub indulges in a constant dance;
the same satiation compels the *agbrerhe** to sing non-stop—

there's a river with divine enabling currents to swim;
there's a moon that spreads a spectacular sheet of pleasure.

Let me dance constantly within like the boneless grub,
let me sing unheard through dawn and dusk like the agbrerhe

because of the beauty I have seen that's so magical
there's no other to compare with the singular bloom.

My feet are on the ground but I feel so high in the clouds
and blown away in a gliding chute of down;

I am here with you but far away in distances unknown,
my wandering has taken an unprecedented turn in the wilds.

Let me dance *odjenema* in a festive garden in my chamber,
let me sing with a birdly voice the world can only imagine

for we have chewed the kernel of a hallucinating nut;
we have taken a dish that leaves no desire for others

now that we possess the secret of joy and share
on a routine basis a divine banquet with birds.

In contentment the grub indulges in a constant dance;
the same satiation compels the agbrerhe to sing non-stop.

69. Occupy Me

You imagine me so misshaped with multiple stomachs in one body
that I am so inhumanly insatiable and always hungry for more,

you imagine what tons of soil can fill the bottomless pit
of my desire of immoderate temper that hurts the earth;

you imagine me a whirlwind that no divine spell slows down
to leave a season of constant calm and beauty of life,

you imagine me a savage blaze of apocryphal proportion
raging blindly to consume dry and green leaves on its way

hence your partisan juror's question of *Mi te ke we-e**?
to nail a bewildered one to the scene of an imaginary crime.

Monsters roam the lone world in the absence of the beloved;
delusions bound to be suffered in the torture house of solitude.

Occupy me like they now do in New York and Lagos
to rid the corporate body of its inordinate greed,

pitch your brazen tent by my heart and maintain total vigil
and allow no wandering thoughts to triumph over you,

you who must carry such placards to embarrass me at all times
so that I know that though one you are really ninety-nine percent

that I shouldn't mess with if I want peace in the world I know.
Do not vandalize my property to spite me for imaginary fears

of every man the world over that's bound to lose his head
in a limitless pool that is a nightmare to the majority.

Leave no space in me for the manicured sirens to fill
with delirious songs that corrupt one to hurt others,

expand to all corners of the known world by all means
that your trademark virtue wields to beat impostor muses

and grow deeper to fill every cell in me with your sweetness
so that I am virtually you and we the same inseparable body.

Wo te ke vwe*! You the diamond in the world of beads!
We know though one the moon outshines countless stars.

Your dish so flavored leaves no desire for any other;
so don't imagine a well however deep without a bottom.

Occupy me to radiate the illumination of your beatitude,
but don't crush me in the dark stampede of a deluded monster.

* *Mi te ke we-e?*: literally in Urhobo, "Am I not enough for you?"
* *Wo te ke vwe!*: in Urhobo, "You are enough for me!"

70. The Challenge

Who assures me of a round hundred percent
challenges me to give out a hundred and ten,

who sings for me the muse's divine melody
asks for my ears totally glued to her voice;

who goes out of her way to offer me a careful gift
wants me however fastidious to display it in my heart,

who crosses my path knowingly or just by accident
knows I too cross hers under fated circumstances;

I have come to know that before something falls
onto my hands, it has been apportioned to me.

Who cries out deeply hurt to have nothing except all
knows well she can more than satiate the other's needs,

who takes me to the highway of freedom teaches me
to obey its traffic lights that should never be violated;

who releases me from the prison house of the police state
offers me the chance to bring down the tyranny in our midst.

And so, who proclaims love for me opens the heart
to a wealth only Olokun gives to pamper her beloved,

who asks for my attention more than caters for me;
who asks for my song provides me its inspiration.

Who brings good news to me shares in the celebration;
who asks for communion wants a share however little.

The muse blesses the minstrel with fortune;
the minstrel adores the muse with praise songs;

when the cherry plant showers fruits on its favorites,
it expects the fortunate one to garner the blessings.

Who colors me bright with love seeks rainbow smiles in return;
who makes record sacrifices for me seeks martyrdom in her faith.